Faith on the Line

The story of James Pratt
(1880-1968)

RAILWAY SIGNALMAN
METHODIST PREACHER
COMMUNITY STALWART
DEVOTED FAMILY MAN

Compiled by John Mollitt

O&U
Onwards & Upwards

Onwards and Upwards Publishers

4 The Old Smithy
London Road
Rockbeare
EX5 2EA
United Kingdom

www.onwardsandupwards.org

Copyright © John Mollitt (2021)

The right of John Mollitt to be identified as the author of this work has been asserted by the author in accordance with the Copyright, Designs and Patents Act 1988.

First edition, published in the United Kingdom by Onwards and Upwards Publishers Ltd. (2021).

ISBN: 978-1-78815-923-4
Typeface: Sabon LT

The views and opinions expressed in this book are the author's own, and do not necessarily represent the views and opinions of Onwards and Upwards Publishers or its staff. Some names and identifying details have been removed to protect the privacy of individuals.

Endorsement

The story of James Pratt, "a railway signalman by occupation but a preacher of the Word by vocation", evokes a sense of a Christian lifestyle and passion that is rarely seen in today's modern world. Modern society has made us product-rich but time-poor. We have time-saving gadgets, computers, smartphones and most have cars, yet we seem to have less time to serve the Lord. The life of James Pratt stands in sharp contrast to our modern way of life. Here was a man, product-poor but time-rich – time well spent in serving and preaching the gospel.

As you read this biography of a life lived in the service of the gospel, you might find yourself inspired to be more committed to reaching people with the gospel and supporting those in the Christian community who can no longer regularly attend their local church meetings.

The challenge of James Pratt's life is this: what legacy will you leave? "…the most valuable legacy we can pass on to our children and grandchildren is not material but spiritual."

The final words of James' final sermon are at the heart of the narrative and encapsulate the passion and drive he had all his life: "If you never remember anything else I've said from this pulpit, remember this: 'Believe on the Lord Jesus Christ, and you will be saved.'"

Liam Johnston
CEO, Railway Mission

Faith on the Line

Contents

Faith on the Line

Foreword

JAMES PRATT WAS A METHODIST LOCAL PREACHER for over seventy years – a striking thing in itself! But of immeasurably greater moment is what he *was* as a preacher. As liberalism was gaining ground and men and churches were moving away from the gospel, James Pratt remained unwaveringly committed to it – from beginning to end. And he lived the gospel as well as preached it. In the Caton, Lancashire community which was his home for much of his life, he was deeply respected for his selflessness, his readiness to help and his frequent visits to those in need. It was his privilege, too, to see the Lord at work in changing people's lives.

It is these things that make *Faith on the Line* so heartening. The period spanned by James Pratt's long life was one of deepening spiritual darkness. Tragically. But the darkness was by no means unbroken. Men like James Pratt, by their faithfulness to the truth, were lights that kept on burning brightly. And here now is his story, rescued from oblivion and written down for our encouragement.

John Mollitt does such a good job of placing his grandfather's preaching ministry in the wider setting of his background and upbringing, his work as a railway signalman, his home, his family, his friends and his service to the community as a local councillor and Justice of the Peace. There is much to interest those who, like me, have an endless fascination for how things were in days gone by. And the book is enriched by a chapter full of sermon outlines that illustrate what a fine preacher James Pratt must have been.

It is a pleasure to have the opportunity to introduce and commend this rewarding read.

David Campbell
Pastor, North Preston Evangelical Church

Introduction

MY GRANDFATHER LIVED FROM 1880 TO 1968 AND IT is almost impossible to visualise the changes he must have witnessed during the course of his life. For example, in the year of his birth, the Elementary Education Act for the first time made education compulsory for five- to ten-year-olds, but by 1964, there was a university in Lancaster, a mere five miles from Granddad's home in Caton. In 1880, there were no cars but within months of his death, man was walking on the moon, whilst steam engines which had dominated the whole of Granddad's working life were withdrawn in 1968. And a UK population of 35 million in 1880 had increased to 55 million in 1968.

In the 1880s, poverty was rife, with any concept of 'cradle to grave' provision still being decades away, Throughout the nineteenth century, England was undoubtedly a Christian country, but by the end of the 1960s, secularism was rampant and any vestige of Victorian moral standards had been replaced by the permissive society.

Some of these changes are touched on in this brief biography, but primarily, it is a personal tribute to a well-loved grandfather and his Christian witness and influence. Granddad, like King David, "served his own generation" – and though his day was very different to our day, may we be encouraged by his example and say with Charles Wesley:

> *To serve the present age,*
> *My calling to fulfil,*

O may it all my powers employ,
To do my Master's will.

I am grateful to my brother Jim Mollitt, to my cousin Jim Pratt and to Andy Souter for valuable information which they have provided in the compiling of this biography.

1

Pen Picture

MY GRANDFATHER, JAMES PRATT, WAS BORN ON 17th April, 1880, at White Birks, Lunds, a small hamlet of widely scattered farms, seven miles from Hawes in North Yorkshire. He was the son of Chris and Mary Pratt and one of ten children, four of whom died in infancy. It was not unusual to be given the name of a predeceased sibling at that time, which is how Granddad came to be called 'James'. A brother, born in 1877, had died when just two weeks old. Records show that Granddad was christened at Hawes Chapel on 16th December, 1880, but in all probability, he was christened at home.

In the year he was born, education became compulsory, and Granddad is to be seen on an 1889 photograph of Lunds School. Being from a farming family, it is open to question just how regular his school attendance might have been. A recently discovered diary of a 1903 Upper Dales school inspector includes a comment on Lunds school: "attendance poor because of the backward harvest". 'Backward' presumably because of the weather.

In 1890, the family made the short move from White Birks Farm to West Rackenthwaite Farm, where their names appear on the 1891 Garsdale census. Granddad then continued and concluded his education at Garsdale School, which is now the village hall.

In October 2019, I took the harvest thanksgiving services at Low Smithy Methodist Church, Garsdale and was entertained by retired farmer Brian Park and his wife in Sedbergh. It was fascinating to learn that they had moved to their retirement bungalow from the very farm where Granddad had been brought up in the 1890s. West Rackenthwaite Farm is now being farmed by their son.

Robert – the only sibling I can recollect – was six years younger from Granddad and, until his death in 1964, lived in Settle, North Yorkshire. In his eighties, Granddad would get the train from Caton to Giggleswick and then walk across the fields to Settle. Robert worshipped at Skipton Road Methodist Church, and I remember preaching there as a young man in 1971.

Interestingly, this invitation to preach came from Willie Preston, who I later learned had remarried after the early death of his first wife, Rose Mary – Granddad's sister. They had married in 1917, but tragically, Rose Mary had died a year later in the great flu epidemic of 1918 when carrying their first child – a sad reminder of how fragile and difficult life could be a hundred years ago. Skipton Road Methodist Church closed in 1979, but thankfully, the building is still a place of worship and is now used by Settle Christian Fellowship.

In the mid and late nineteenth century, the area around Sedbergh, Garsdale and Dent suffered depression in agriculture, and several farmers left the area and moved to Liverpool. Among these were Chris and Mary Pratt who, in 1894, moved to West Derby. Here, they started up a dairy to supply the increasing population with fresh milk. The move was aided by the opening of the Settle to Carlisle railway in 1876, which made the transporting of people and cattle so much easier. And so, at the age of fourteen, James Pratt transferred from the country to the emerging city.

In Liverpool, the 'cow-keepers' – as they were known – purchased end terraced properties with a side entrance to a backyard. Here, the cows were kept and fed on grass harvested from the city parks and playing fields. Some of the grass cuttings were gathered by children from the land surrounding Goodison Park – the home of Everton FC. This resulted in Granddad becoming a 'Toffee' supporter, and he often recalled delivering milk near the football ground. Many years later, preaching in the open-air outside Goodison Park, I must have been standing where the feet of Granddad had once trodden.

It was, however, arduous work, as the cows had to be milked at 5 a.m. and 3 p.m., and there were milk rounds at 7 a.m. and 4 p.m. Milk churns were used, with milk being measured into the customer's jug at the door. In between, the cows had to be cleaned, bedding replaced and the milk churns scolded. At the turn of the twentieth century, five hundred premises – known as cowhouses – were licensed to keep cows.

The 'cow keepers' were largely considered 'foreigners', as the natives did not find it easy to understand the dialect. They were, however, a closely knit community with chapel-going and social activities remaining strong. There was some inter-marriage, but many returned to the Dales to find their life partner.

In Merseyside, the Pratt sojourn was relatively short and not without sadness, as two more children died in infancy. Within four years, Chris and Mary had returned to Yorkshire, buying a farm in Settle. Granddad did not return with them, and in 1899, he joined the railways as a signal lamp man at Barnsley. Oil lamps that illuminated signals needed to be changed each day – come rain or shine. The lamp man would climb a ladder, and whilst at times it afforded great views, in winter with slippery steps, howling gales and teeming rain, it could be a hazardous occupation.

Barnsley was to be followed by stints as a station porter at Cudworth, Kildwick, Crosshills and Ryston before Granddad was promoted to porter signalman at Earby. In 1905, he was appointed as a signalman at Thornton in Craven, and in June 1906, he transferred to Caton, where he stayed for thirty-nine years until his retirement in 1945. His career spanned the two world wars, but he was never called up for active service due to railway work being a reserved occupation.

I used to wonder why the son of a Dales farmer should be attracted to the railways but I think there is an obvious explanation. In May 1876 – four years before Granddad was born – the Settle to Carlisle line had opened. The railways had come to Garsdale, and it is perhaps not impossible to imagine the impact this development must have had on an isolated, rural area.

As a young boy, Granddad would have worshipped at Hawes Junction Methodist Chapel, and this building had a direct link with the Midland Railway. The foundation stone was laid the day the Settle to Carlisle line opened, and the stonemasons who built the chapel had also built Garsdale station. The chapel was painted in the colours of the Midland Railway and is believed to be the only place of worship ever to have been built by a railway contractor.

Lunds school, where Granddad was first educated, opened in 1878 and was originally specifically for the children of railwaymen. Therefore, from his earliest years, Granddad must have been familiar with the railways, and I have no doubt this was a factor in his working life being spent as a signalman.

Granddad retired before I was born and so I never saw him in his working environment. A decade later, his signal box at Caton was destroyed by fire, when it was set alight by a spark from a passing engine. The signal box was replaced by a new brick building, but its life was short, as by 1967 the line had closed.

His work life, however, was not confined to the railways because sometimes, on his day off, he would travel twenty-five miles to help his son with farm work. Here, he would turn his hand to dry stone walling – a skill he had learned as a boy in Garsdale. Even retirement did not mean cessation from work, as he worked twice a week with his son, who now had a poultry business.

Granddad met and courted a Hawes girl – Mary Elizabeth Eglin – and married her at Nether Kellet Congregational Church in 1907. They had three children, six grandchildren, and celebrated their diamond wedding in 1967. By this time, Grandma was too frail for any organised celebration, but ten years earlier, I remember being at their golden wedding when a family meal was held at a café in Caton.

My only recollection of the day is listening to the FA Cup final. The game was between Aston Villa and Manchester United, and it is the first cup final I ever remember. Knowing Granddad's interest in football, he may have been faced with the dilemma many have encountered since – attending a family function but wanting to be kept informed of what is happening at Wembley Stadium!

For many years, Grandma had indifferent health and Granddad devotedly nursed and cared for her. There was just one occasion when it became obvious he needed a rest, and so Grandma came to our home, and Granddad went to stay with his son and wife at Over Kellet. Latterly, a Christian neighbour came each evening to help Grandma to bed, whilst church members often sat with her on a Sunday, so that Granddad could get to a service.

Thankfully, they remained together in their own home until Granddad was hospitalised. No doubt, caring for Grandma had taken its toll on his health, and a stroke meant he was taken into Lancaster Moor Hospital. He was an excellent patient, but his body was 'worn out', and at the age of eighty-eight, he passed into glory.

His funeral service was held at Quernmore Methodist Church on the Saturday before Christmas. It would not have been possible to accommodate the numbers wishing to attend in Granddad's home church of Brookhouse. Indeed, such were the numbers that police were on duty, directing the traffic on Caton's back road to Quernmore. The snowy conditions did not prevent the church from being packed to capacity.

The service was led by the superintendent minister of the Lancaster Methodist circuit and the tribute given by an old family friend, Mr Isaac Towers of Halton. Isaac himself was not in good health but determined to take part in the service. Movingly, he began his tribute by emphasising he would not have done it for anyone else but Mr Pratt. He then proceeded to say that though Granddad might not have been considered great in the eyes of the world, he possessed true greatness – greatness in the kingdom of God.

Grandma could not visit Granddad in the hospital or be at his funeral; nevertheless, her final memory of him was a happy one. In later weeks, she would often recall how, as he was wheeled out of 43 Hornby Road to the ambulance, Granddad had smiled and given her a cheerful wave.

The interment was in the graveyard at Quernmore Methodist Church – the resting place of many local believers, and it was here that Grandma joined him after her passing in March 1971. A great reunion of many of the Lord's people can be joyfully anticipated when the trumpet sounds and Jesus comes again.

2

Lay Preaching

CHRIS PRATT – GRANDDAD'S FATHER – CAME FROM Congregational stock, but having been converted in a Dales revival, he became a Primitive Methodist. At that time, the preaching of Richard Atkinson, known as the 'Apostle of the Dales', was having a significant impact on the spiritual life of the area.

Richard, a gamekeeper, lived on the borders of Garsdale and Grisedale – a dale which, through the TV documentary *Grisedale: the Dale that Died*, gained a measure of fame in the 1970s. The local church – long since converted into a home – was known as the Richard Atkinson Memorial Chapel.

A service was held at White Birks farm every Sunday afternoon at 2 p.m., and on moving to West Rackenthwaite, the family worshipped at Garsdale Street Primitive Methodist Church, and it was here that Granddad was converted. My cousin can recall preaching at 'The Street' over fifty years ago and an elderly lady telling him how, as a young teenager, Granddad had come to the penitent form.

It was therefore with the Primitive Methodists that at the age of sixteen, Granddad began to preach, and the same lady could still remember his first faltering attempt. The Garsdale Street chapel was full, and Granddad, shy and hesitant, confessed, "I'm not much of a public speaker." "Needn't tell them that," responded one of his great uncles. "It'll soon become obvious."

The starting point for becoming a 'Prims' preacher was the conversion experience, characterised by a conviction of sin and then, through Christ, an assurance of God's forgiveness. Having had this life-changing experience, converts had a desire to tell others, which led some to local preaching. The first stage was to go on the preaching plan as an 'Exhorter'. This involved giving testimony in a worship service under the watchful eye of an experienced preacher. Later, the trainee would proceed to take a text and expound upon it.

Before being accepted as a Local Preacher, three questions were addressed by the Primitive Methodist Church to the candidate.

1. *Has he grace?*
   This addressed his conversion experience, the life he was now living and his devotion to the will of God.

2. *Has he gifts as well as graces?*
   This addressed his knowledge, understanding and interpretation of the scriptures and also his ability to express biblical truth clearly and persuasively.

3. *Has he fruit?*
   What evidence is there that people have been converted to God under his ministry?

Persons who ticked these boxes were deemed fit to preach and went onto a full plan. To maintain their status, preachers had to attend class meetings and fulfil plan appointments regularly. Granddad met the required criteria and thus began a ministry that would take him thousands of miles and to hundreds of chapels.

Some seventy years after the Primitive Methodists accepted Granddad to be a preacher, I was accepted by the Methodist denomination. The practical training was like that of the 'Prims' as I began 'on note', announcing the hymns and doing the Bible readings for an accredited preacher, before proceeding to being 'on trial', which meant I was now able to take an entire service.

However, I do not recall the three questions addressed by the Primitive Methodists ever being put to me. The emphasis instead seemed to be on the Local Preacher's exam. While I do not underestimate the importance of theological training, this should never be at the expense of personal testimony and character.

Granddad knew this, and an incident stands out when he was holidaying with us in Morecambe. The preacher on the Sunday morning was a ministerial training student, but what Granddad really thought of him only became apparent when it was time for the evening service. On being asked, "Are you going to the service?" he replied, "No, I will stop and read the *Christian Herald* to mother – there is more gospel in there than you will get tonight." He always regretted the 'Prims' joining the 'Wesleyans' in 1923, as he felt this marked a decline in adherence to biblical truth and gospel preaching.

Granddad would have left school by the age of twelve, but I was impressed by his spiritual depth and understanding of biblical truth when reading his sermon notes. Charles H. Spurgeon wrote:

> *I do not know a nobler occupation for a man than*
> *for him to be maintaining himself by his shop or*

whatever else his calling may be, and going out to suburban villages on the Sabbath to preach. There ought to be more who seek to improve their minds, that they may preach acceptably anywhere the gospel of Jesus Christ. If you cannot edify a thousand, yet you can preach a sermon here and there, and tell to different companies the same story of the Saviour's love.

Here, in a nutshell, is a picture of my grandfather – a railway signalman by occupation but a preacher of the Word by vocation.

At least on two occasions, he was invited to pastor churches. One of the churches was in Lincolnshire and the other in Texas, North America. As Grandma had never travelled farther afield than Liverpool, there was no possibility of the family moving to Lincolnshire, never mind North America.

Granddad never owned a car but had a bicycle, an autocycle and later a motorbike. These were his mode of transport, and it enabled him to take preaching appointments not just in his own circuit but in circuits as far away as Settle, Garstang, Sedbergh and Kendal. My mother recalled how it was not unusual for him to set out before eight in the morning and not to return until after ten at night.

With most preachers having cars today, we give little thought to a previous generation of preachers who were dependant on public transport, bicycles or even 'Shanks' pony' to get them to their appointments. I have only twice cycled to preaching engagements and the second occasion was the last. What I imagined to be a leisurely ride turned out to be as demanding as any stage of the Tour de France. I arrived at the church so exhausted and out of breath that whilst I managed to announce the opening hymn, there was no way I could sing it. I cannot but admire my grandfather and many others who must have arrived at services cold, wet and tired.

Granddad's preaching was not confined to Methodism, and he often officiated at Baptist and Congregational churches. Caton Baptist was a church which held a special significance for him because it was here that he was baptised as a believer Apparently, he ran home still dripping in his wet clothes.

Extracts from the *Lancaster Guardian* archives reveal he was also in demand at Holiness Mission churches:

> *A special service was held on Good Friday at the Bowerham Holiness Mission when Mr. J. Pratt of Caton gave a Bible address on 'The Cross'.*
>
> *22 April 1938*

> *The Carnforth Pentecostal Holiness Mission held their annual Sunday School Prizegiving on Sunday, when the preacher was Mr. J. Pratt of Caton.*
>
> *31 March 1939*

> *The Main Street Holiness Mission, Skerton held their harvest festival at the weekend. On the Monday evening, the speaker was Mr. J. Pratt of Caton.*
>
> *10 October 1941*

Granddad also had a long association with the Independent Methodist Church in Lancaster, and in March 1968, he took part in a special service.

> *A re-dedication service to mark the completion of renovations at the Independent Methodist Church, Nelson Street, Lancaster, drew a large inter-*

denominational congregation to the church on Monday evening. The speaker was Mr. John Pratt of Over Kellet who, for over thirty years, has served the church as a visiting preacher. Mr. James Pratt Senior of Caton also played a great part in the service. It was a big occasion for him as he too has served the church as a visiting preacher for more than fifty years. The chairman was Mr. James Pratt of Hale. He, like his father and grandfather, has served the church in the same capacity.

Lancaster Guardian, March 1968

This was to be Granddad's last service at the Independent Methodist Church, as he was to die some nine months later. It is possible he knew he would never preach at the church again, for he finished with these memorable words: "If you never remember anything else I've said from this pulpit, remember this: 'Believe on the Lord Jesus Christ, and you will be saved.'"

The only time I can recall hearing Granddad preach was at this particular church when he was on holiday with us in Morecambe. He was now in his eighties, and we had an early morning walk to catch the bus into Lancaster. This was followed by another three-quarter-mile walk to the church. He preached on the feeding of the five thousand, and after the service, we made the reverse journey back to Morecambe. Looking through Granddad's preaching notes, I was interested in finding his outline for this particular sermon.

In retirement, Granddad was much in demand to speak at afternoon Ladies' Meetings. I understand he used to begin by saying, "I've brought a woman with me, and it is not my wife." He would then speak about Ruth, Esther, Mary, Martha or some other biblical woman.

23

Granddad used to lecture on well-known believers, and I have his notes on Fanny Crosby, Lax of Poplar and Samuel Chadwick. They make fascinating reading. For example, Fanny Crosby – the blind author of some 9,000 hymns – wrote her first poem when she was just eight years of age:

> *O, what a happy child I am*
> *Although I cannot see.*
> *I am resolved that in the world*
> *Contented I shall be.*
> *How many blessings I enjoy*
> *That other people don't.*
> *To weep or sigh because I'm blind*
> *I cannot nor I won't.*

William Henry Lax was a Lancashire lad who was the Superintendent of the Poplar and Bow Mission for twenty-five years. Mayor of Poplar in 1918-1919, he met George V on three occasions. When he was born, his mother hugged, kissed him and said, "Let him live to preach Thy Word. Let him to Thy glory live. His every sacred moment spend. In publishing the sinner's friend." The mother's prayer was abundantly answered, although she was never to see it, as she died when William was still a young boy.

Samuel Chadwick, a Principal of Cliff College, was one of Granddad's spiritual 'heroes'. He too was a Lancashire lad, born in 1860 into a two-bedroomed terraced house in Burnley. By the age of eight, he was rising at 6 a.m. to work with his father in the cotton mill. Converted as a child, he would later rush home after a twelve-hour shift for five hours of study and prayer.

As a member of Brookhouse Methodist Church, Granddad represented the church at other services and events. Each November for many years, he read the lesson at the Service of Remembrance held at St. Paul's Church, Brookhouse. Two further extracts from the *Lancaster Guardian* of 1942 illustrate other services in which he participated:

> *Representatives of Moor Lane Methodist Circuit assembled at Skerton Main Street Methodist Church last evening week to honour Mr. George Armistead of Bolton le Sands who has completed fifty years as a local preacher. Mr. James Pratt (Brookhouse) described journeys they had made together to preaching appointments.*
>
> Lancaster Guardian, June 1942

My mother could recall Mr. Armistead arriving at Brookhouse on horseback – a mode of transport much favoured by John Wesley.

> *The Rev. C. Corjus, the new minister of Nelson Street (Lancaster) and Caton Baptist Church was formally welcomed by the officers and members of the churches. Mr. James Pratt welcomed the Rev. Corjus on behalf of the Methodist Church.*
>
> Lancaster Guardian, August 1942

During his lifetime, Granddad often ministered at funerals as the following indicate:

> *The funeral service of Mrs. —— of Rock M' Jock, Caton took place yesterday. A short service was conducted at the house by the Rev. L.A. Thomas and*

> *Mr. J. Pratt, prior to the internment at Brookhouse churchyard.*
>
> *Lancaster Guardian, June 1939*

> *The funeral service of Mr. —— took place at High Bentham Methodist Church on Wednesday. One of his lay preaching colleagues, Mr. J. Pratt of Caton paid a glowing tribute to the work of Mr. ——.*
>
> *Lancaster Guardian, November 1954*

As an ex-Primitive Methodist, Granddad was a frequent speaker at Camp Meetings. In the *Methodist Preachers' Who's Who* for 1934, "preaching at camp meetings" was listed as one of his interests. The first such meeting in England was held at Mow Cop in North Staffordshire on Sunday, 31st May, 1807. Further such meetings, characterised by fervent singing, praying and preaching were held, but when judged as being "highly improper" by the Wesleyan Methodist Conference, it resulted in the birth of the Primitive Methodist Connexion.

> *Fine weather favoured the annual camp meeting held at Hill Crest, Brookhouse (by kind permission of Mr. Mason) on Sunday afternoon and evening. The preachers were Messrs. T. Harper and W. Preston of Sedbergh and Mr. J. Pratt of Caton. Collections were in aid of the Royal Lancaster Infirmary.*
>
> *Lancaster Guardian, 24 June 1938*

In 1972, I was privileged to preach with my uncle at the Brookhouse Camp Meeting, but by then, such meetings were beginning to lose their appeal. It was, nevertheless, a memorable experience, preaching in a barn from a horse cart to a congregation seated on bales of hay.

Granddad was an active member of the Methodist Local Preacher's Mutual Aid Association. The LPMA commenced in 1849 as a charity providing financial and other assistance to Methodist and Wesleyan Reform Local Preachers and their families. It proved to be a lifeline for many, but as welfare provision through the state became more comprehensive, there was less call on charities to provide for those in financial need. Consequently, it was superseded by the formation of a new charity in 2005, still providing financial support but also preaching resources, information etc., for preachers and leaders of worship.

As a boy, I remember that the Sunday after Easter was always LPMA Sunday, and on this day, local preachers from other circuits occupied the pulpits. Offerings were for LPMA, and the Sunday served as a rest day for ministers after the busyness of Easter week.

Mr. James Pratt of Caton was elected president of the Lancaster and District branch of the Methodist Local Preacher's Mutual Aid Association meeting held at the Sulyard Street Methodist Church.

Lancaster Guardian, 11 March 1949

Amongst my grandfather's papers, I discovered an interesting letter dated 1st November, 1962, from the Rev. F.A. Kinchin of Bentham:

Dear Mr. Pratt

One of our Low Bentham members, Mr. —— passed away in Lancaster Infirmary, this morning. As you are planned at Low Bentham next Sunday, I thought you would wish to know about this bereavement

27

and you would desire to remember the family in your prayers. Perhaps you could choose a hymn that would be appropriate to their need.

God bless you, as you minister the Word of Life next Sunday.

With cordial greetings.

When I moved to Ingleton in 1979, local Methodists still spoke with affection of Rev. Kinchin and his pastoral heart – the pastoral heart revealed in the above correspondence. The letter also shows how different things were in the 1960s compared with today – no e-mails, no text messages, and my grandparents were not on the phone. So, there was no alternative to 'snail mail'. Information which can now be dispatched in a moment would then have taken a day or two. Perhaps Granddad had no time to respond before the Sunday, but I have no doubt he reacted positively to the request.

Quoting George Whitfield, Granddad often said he wanted to "wear out, not rust out", and his wish was fulfilled. He was still preaching at the age of eighty-eight but now accompanied to services by my uncle. This was not just because he needed transport, but because on one occasion, he had lost his thoughts and begun to ramble.

I remember one Sunday morning at Ingleton when a well-known preacher had a similar experience. He was devastated as it had never happened before, and he put it down to having had "too many birthdays". After a good rest in the afternoon, he preached at the evening service with his customary clarity and power.

I have not had access to them, but I understand that Granddad kept notebooks in which he recorded details of his preaching ministry. These included not only the date, the place and the number present, but also the liberty he had felt and the response of the congregation. When staying with us in Morecambe, I do recall him saying, "It is twenty years tonight since Mrs. —— was converted." I assume he must have been looking back at one of his notebooks.

Shortly before he died, Granddad was presented with a seventy-year preaching certificate in the hospital. This went with the fifty-year service certificate he had received at Moor Lane Methodist Church in October 1948. The fifty-year certificate is in my possession and has inscribed upon it the dying words of John Wesley: "The best of all is, God is with us."

Seventy years as a preacher is a remarkable achievement but even more so because it was characterised by faithfulness and fervour. Sadly, he lived through days when many preachers departed from biblical truth, but Granddad never did and with Charles Wesley was...

Happy if with my latest breath
I may but gasp His Name,
Preach Him to all and cry in death,
"Behold, behold the Lamb."

3

Faithful Visitor

IN THE ALREADY REFERRED TO *METHODIST PREACH-ers' Who's Who* of 1934, some of James Pratt's interests are stated as "visiting the aged, sick, infirm and lonely". The Bible clearly indicates that this interest should be characteristic of all true believers. The Apostle James wrote, "Pure and undefiled religion before God and the Father is this: to visit orphans and widows in their trouble, and to keep oneself unspotted from the world."[1] Jesus said, "I was sick and you visited Me ... inasmuch as you did it to one of the least of these My brethren, you did it to Me."[2]

Granddad's visitation in Caton was legendary, with every Monday and Thursday in retirement being devoted to calling at homes in the village. As with his Master, no task was too lowly or demeaning, and so shopping, gardening, chopping wood, setting fires and practical help in the home went hand in hand with prayer and scripture reading.

Indeed, such was his standing in the village that when a local doctor felt he could do no more for a patient, his advice would be, "Go and see Mr Pratt." In today's culture of political correctness, any doctor now making any such suggestion would be in danger of being struck off.

---

[1] James 1:27
[2] Matthew 25:36,40

This doctor was not the notorious Dr Buck Ruxton who was found guilty of murdering his wife and housemaid and, in 1936, was hanged at Strangeways prison, Manchester. Dr Ruxton had his practice in Lancaster but held surgeries in Caton, where he was popular and well respected in the village. He was known as a diligent and compassionate physician who on occasions waived his treatment fees when he felt that a patient was too poor to pay them. My grandfather and Dr Ruxton – two esteemed men in the Caton community, but sadly, how different their lives turned out to be.

Amongst Granddad's papers, I came across the following interesting observations which illustrate that, for him, visiting was always a two-way thing:

> *Miss A.E. Died 1957. Aged 48. To visit her was a blessing. Her faith was in Jesus, and everyone who visited during her illness benefited.*

> *Miss L.S. Died Dec. 1948. L. was converted in August 1925, and her whole ambition was to serve Jesus. She was very shy at first, but the Holy Spirit took away fear.*

> *Mrs N. Died July 1963. Losing her husband in 1949, she was very poor but very humble. Visited her weekly for 14 years or more, and there were many times of blessing.*

In the 'Acknowledgements' section of the *Lancaster Guardian*, Granddad was from time to time thanked for his faithful visitation:

The family of the late Mr. H wish to thank Mr J. Pratt who through the years has given of his time and companionship.

Lancaster Guardian, 1955

Up to the age of eighty-six, my grandparents spent the day with us in Morecambe every Wednesday, but for Granddad it was not a break from visiting. On the contrary, after lunch, he would catch the 13.15 bus to Heysham, which was at the other end of the town. Calling first at the home of my great auntie, he then proceeded to walk the four miles back to our home. As he did so, he would visit ministers, lay preachers and others who lived in Morecambe – some of whom had retired to the town. These included some ex-Prims who had preached with him on the Lancaster Circuit.

A stickler for time, it was almost always on the stroke of 16.45 when Granddad came through the door, sometimes wet and often a little pale through the exertion of the walk. He would then warm himself by the fire and report back to us on those he had visited.

Amongst these was the Rev. James Dinsdale, who was born in Gayle, the next village to Hawes, in the same year as my grandfather. After his father's early death, James settled with his widowed mother in Nelson and worked in a cotton mill. On entering the Methodist ministry, he served for seven years as a missionary in the West Indies, followed by eight circuits in the UK, before retiring to Morecambe in 1946.

His obituary from the minutes of the Methodist Conference 1962 perhaps explains why my grandfather had such an affinity with him:

He delighted to proclaim the message of full redemption. In him, everything was subordinated to his life's great passion: to preach the Gospel and the saving grace of Jesus Christ. He was a man whom to know was to love.

My personal recollection of Rev. James Dinsdale is also of his evangelistic zeal. During the summer season, as he walked to church on a Sunday morning, he would enquire of holidaymakers reading their newspapers on the promenade, "Have you read your Bible this morning?" Who can tell the impact such a question might have had upon a wandering soul?

Another port of call was the home of Mr F.G. Doubikin, who, as an elderly man, I remember preaching at my church in Morecambe. He was an interesting character for, as a businessman, he used his material prosperity to finance gospel work. Supporting a full-time evangelist, together they conducted missions – week one, Mr Doubikin would 'sow the seed'; and week two, the evangelist would 'reap the harvest'.

He also visited Mr A.T. Humble – a retired headmaster – and I recall Granddad recounting an amusing letter which Mr Humble had once received from a church secretary:

As you are the preacher next Sunday night, I am writing to let you know that we have cancelled the service.

The secretary was given the benefit of the doubt, that he had expressed himself badly and it was not a comment on Mr Humble's preaching!

Granddad did not have an extroverted personality, being by nature somewhat reserved. What then made him such a welcomed visitor? Like many of his generation, he had a genuine interest in people. Today, with twenty-four-hour news, we know what is happening anywhere in the world, almost as it occurs. This was not the case during my grandfather's lifetime, and so local news and local people were the focus of his attention.

Granddad was also a good listener, and to be a welcomed visitor, this is an essential qualification. It has been rightly said, "We have two ears and one mouth, and it is best to use them in that proportion." This is more than just good human advice, as it is advocated in the Bible. "He who answers a matter before he hears it, it is a folly and shame to him."[3] "Let every man be swift to hear, slow to speak."[4]

However, in his visitation, Granddad had an overriding motivation, perhaps best expressed in Charles Wesley's words, "O let me commend my Saviour to you." This he sought to do, not by 'forcing the gospel down anyone's throat', for this can be counterproductive, but rather by sympathetic listening, an encouraging word, scripture reading and intercessory prayer.

[3] Proverbs 18:13
[4] James 1:19

4

Brookhouse Methodist

THERE WERE TWO METHODIST CHURCHES WITHIN reach of Granddad's house, but whilst Caton was just around the corner, Brookhouse was a mile away. However, before Methodist Union in 1932, Caton had been Wesleyan and Brookhouse, Primitive, and this explains why for over sixty years, Brookhouse Methodist Church was his spiritual home.

I remember once accompanying Granddad on his regular Saturday evening walk to Brookhouse. Once inside the church, he switched on the heat, wound up the clock and got the hymn books out of a cupboard, ready for the morning Sunday School. That night has remained with me as a reminder that the Lord sees and will reward all service done in secret. As pastors and preachers, our ministry is inevitably 'seen of men', but may we ever be kept from that pharisaic spirit so condemned by Christ.

Granddad's busy preaching schedule meant there were Sundays when he could not be at Brookhouse, and yet his commitment to the local church could never be doubted. Society Steward, Sunday School Superintendent, Trustees Secretary and Leader of Christian Endeavour – these were just some of the offices he conscientiously held for many years.

In August 1961, special centenary services were held at the church, and Granddad was the preacher at both services on the opening Sunday. He later chaired the Centenary Meeting on

Tuesday, 29th August. An anniversary leaflet was produced, stating in the foreword:

> It is to Mr. James Pratt, still happily with us after more than fifty years' devoted service, that we are indebted for the account which follows.

His account begins with a report from the *Primitive Methodist Magazine* of October 1861:

> At Brookhouse, Lancaster Mission, we have recently built a Connexional Chapel. The foundation stone was laid on Good Friday and the opening services took place on Sundays 7th and 14th July. It is a neat and substantial building in a good situation about the centre of the village. The total cost is about £100, towards which we have raised nearly £50. May the Lord make this sanctuary a great blessing to the place and in it may many souls be saved.

Granddad then proceeds with a brief history of the church:

> The passing years have brought many changes. A new organ was bought in 1907. Electric lighting was installed in October 1931, and electric heating in October 1941. A kitchen and toilets were added in 1961.
>
> A morning Sunday School commenced in 1915 and continues still. The Christian Endeavour Society started in 1907, remaining a centre of devotion and a good training ground for Christian service. There were nine lads on "Young People's Day" in 1922 who accepted Christ as their Saviour. One of these became a Minister of Religion; three became local

preachers, one a church organist, another a Cliff College evangelist and one the pastor of a Mission. The prayer for souls to be saved, offered at the opening of the church, has not gone unanswered.

Today, the opportunity presented by a growing village is accepted as a challenge by a vigorous society, whose hope and confidence lie not in their own resources but in the God and Father of our Lord Jesus Christ.

Joseph Huddleston was the young man who went on to pastor Ayres Quay Mission in Sunderland, and in 1961, as part of the Centenary celebrations, a booklet was produced, telling the story of his short life. In it, the author – Arnold Hornsby – gives more details of the 'Young People's Day' when Joseph and the other young men were converted:

That occasion in October 1922, was an important milestone in Joseph's life. It became a great and memorable day with other young people, too. James Pratt, the Superintendent of Brookhouse Sunday School, spent much time in prayer about his scholars. On this particular day, the lads turned up in a very strong force. The message was based on the great challenge of Joshua to the Children of Israel – "Choose you this day whom you will serve, as for me and my house, we will serve the Lord." The closing words of the address were – "What is going to be your choice today?"

Young Joseph stepped to the front, and in the simple and clear language of a country lad, he made the

> *greatest choice of his life to serve God with all his heart and soul and mind. Eight companions joined him. In the attitude of prayer, they knelt together and with great joy, their beloved Superintendent pointed them to their Lord and Saviour, Jesus Christ. A truly remarkable answer to prayer.*

From childhood, Joseph knew indifferent health but after training at Cliff College, he was called to pastor a mission church in Sunderland. His ministry was to be fruitful but short, and at the early age of thirty-seven, he was called to his heavenly home. The booklet *Greatheart of Littledale (shepherd of the sheep to pastor of the flock)* concludes with the moving words of my grandfather:

> *The last time I saw Joe was on my visit to Pott Yeats on Wednesday 17th December 1941, when we both took part in a Christian Endeavour meeting. Afterwards, we walked together to our respective homes for about a quarter of a mile where we parted, little thinking that we should not meet again in the flesh. He took the road to the right to Bell Hill Farm and I took the road to the left to Caton. Shortly afterwards, I heard that he had gone to Sunderland and then, there came news of his illness. I prayed that it was the Lord's will that he might be spared for further work for his Master, but evidently, his work was finished, and he was translated to higher service on 31st January, 1942.*

> *On a bitterly cold, snowbound afternoon, a large congregation came to the funeral at Quernmore. Some said it was more like a revival service than a*

funeral. Truly the Lord was in the midst to bless and to help. On the following Sunday, a Memorial Service was held at Pott Yeats, when about sixty people attended. I spoke from John 11:37, and we felt the real Presence of our Lord Jesus Christ. To God be the glory for such a life lived in His service.

The old Methodist building where Joseph was converted is now a private house, but a new church was opened on the site of a former garage in 1995. However, I did have the privilege of occupying the pulpit where Granddad had so often preached when I took the Monday evening harvest thanksgiving service in 1984.

I remember this service, but not for the noblest of reasons. Before the service, I went to the toilet and to my dismay, I found that the zip on my trousers had gone. This caused no problem whilst I was in the pulpit, but when I shook hands at the door, all I could do was fasten my jacket and hope that it would cover my embarrassment.

In his lapel, Granddad sported a CE badge – the emblem of Christian Endeavour. This interdenominational Christian youth society was formed in 1881 in the United States and expanded rapidly, growing from a single church group into a world movement. By 1906, there were 67,000 Christian Endeavour societies worldwide, with over four million members.

The Society's aims were expressed in the Christian Endeavour pledge:

Trusting in the Lord Jesus Christ for strength, I promise Him that I will do whatever He would like to have me do; that I will make it the rule of my life

> *to pray and to read the Bible every day, and to support the work and worship of my own church in every way possible; and that just as far as I know how, through my whole life, I will endeavour to lead a Christian life.*

> *As an active member, I promise to be true to all my duties, to be present and to take some part, aside from singing, in every Christian Endeavour meeting, unless hindered by some reason which I can conscientiously give my Lord and Master, Jesus Christ. If obliged to be absent from the monthly consecration meeting of the society, I will, if possible, send at least a verse of Scripture to be read in response to my name at the roll call.*

Granddad first became acquainted with Christian Endeavour in 1896 at Hawes Congregational Church, and on marriage in 1907, he helped to form the society at Brookhouse Methodist Church. The group began with ten members and was still going strong when Granddad spoke at the Brookhouse CE Jubilee in November 1957. I have the notes which he used on that occasion:

> *CE – what the letters do not mean. Cash Expected. Census Explained. Courting Encouraged.*

> *CE – what the letters may mean.*

> *1) Conversion Essential;*
> *2) Conscience Eased;*
> *3) Conduct Enabled;*
> *4) Character Enriched;*
> *5) Consecration Experienced;*

6) *Communion Enjoyed;*
7) *Conflicts Encountered;*
8) *Christ Enthroned;*
9) *Coronation Expected.*

Pat and I have cause to be thankful to Christian Endeavour, as it was at a CE meeting at Heysham Methodist Church in 1970 that we first met. Until we were married, we were regular attenders at the Monday evening meeting and, as young believers, were helped both by the teaching we received and the fellowship we enjoyed.

In 2013 and 2014, I was privileged to speak at the Christian Endeavour UK autumn break at Cardiff's Hebron Hall. They were mainly elderly folk – some in their nineties – but they were enthusiastic believers and many testified how, when first converted, Christian Endeavour had grounded them in the faith. Today, with other Christian organisations having come to the fore, the movement is now relatively weak in the UK.

5

Trade Union Official JP Parish Councillor

MEN OF MY GRANDDAD'S GENERATION DID NOT have the same leisure time enjoyed by many today. Longer working hours, family responsibilities, church commitments and preaching engagements meant that time for hobbies and other interests was limited. However, outside of work, home and church, Granddad did pursue other things.

On his retirement from the railway in 1945, Granddad had been a member of the National Union of Railwaymen (NUR) for over forty years, having served the Wennington branch as chairman for twenty-six years and secretary for six years. To mark his retirement, he was presented with a barometer, and members...

> ...*spoke in appreciative terms of Mr. Pratt's connection with the union, paying tribute to his sterling character.*
>
> Lancaster Guardian, 1946

Primitive Methodism made a significant contribution to the origin and development of trade unions. Most adherents were overwhelmingly working-class, and between 1874 and 1932, forty-four MPs were members of, or closely associated with, the church. In addition, eighty Primitive Methodists were employed as full-time trade union officials.

To appreciate the interconnection between Granddad's faith, his work as a signalman and his trade union involvement, it is helpful to quote from an article written by the Rev. F.S. Bullough in the *Christian Messenger* of 1921:

> *The railwayman is a type distinct. He has responsibilities that sober him and privileges of which he is keenly jealous. He lives in a world altogether peculiar and is conscious of a comradeship within that world which is often warm and generous. Our church (Primitive Methodism) has gained much from the loyalty and devotion of railway servants. The solid qualities of these men have been a great asset in our upbuilding. Local preachers have occupied the footplate and signalman have been found in the class meeting. Railwaymen's Mission Bands have been formed and even Railwaymen's Camp Meetings have been held.*
>
> *From the earliest days of Trade Unionism, our men have taken their share of responsibility. The ideals of mutual help and sick benefit held a strong appeal to our men, whose moral passion was kindled at Calvary. As a church, we owe great gratitude to railway workers of all grades. To these brave and humble Primitive Methodists who took Christ into the signal cabin or were loyal to him on the footplate.*

This resonates with me, as I remember my mother recalling how Granddad not only prepared sermons at work but on occasions, in the signal box, he would have a prayer meeting with one of the porters. This was when work would allow and, of course, long before the days of political correctness and Health and Safety initiatives. However, it does illustrate that Granddad took 'Christ into the signal cabin' and that, for him, there was no separation of the 'sacred' and the 'secular'.

The first record I have of his union activity comes from a newspaper report in 1908:

> *The annual parade of the Carnforth branch of the Amalgamated Society of Railway Servants took place yesterday afternoon. The processionists attended a service at the Co-operative Hall conducted by Mr J. Pratt of Caton. A collection was taken on behalf of the society's orphan fund.*
>
> *Lancashire Evening Post, 8 June 1908*

The ASRS was a trade union for railway workers between 1872 and 1913, which then merged with other unions to form the NUR (National Union of Railway Workers).

Besides his commitment to the trade union movement, Granddad was, for many years, a member of both Caton Parish Council and Lunesdale District Council; on occasions, being chairman of both bodies. In 1946, on being elected to the council, his letter of thanks to the electors of Caton with Littledale appeared in the paper:

> *I wish to express my thanks to you for once again electing me as one of your representatives on the District Council and trust that I may be able to serve your interests to the best of my ability.*
>
> *Lancaster Guardian, 1946*

Reports from the *Lancaster Guardian* of 1938 and 1939 illustrate the kind of matters that Granddad was involved in as a parish councillor:

> *A letter was read from the Coronation Planting Committee, relating to the planting of a tree in the village, in commemoration of the King's access to the throne.*
>
> *18 February 1938*

> *Attention was drawn to the fact that street lighting had been recently going out at 10.30 pm on some evenings instead of 11.15 pm.*
>
> *03 March 1939*

> *The Poor Land account showed a balance of £8.10s.6d. Forty people receiving 4s.6d each from the fund at Christmas.*
>
> *31 March 1939*

> *Some discussion took place concerning the formation of a Local Authority Fire Brigade.*
>
> *22 September 1939*

Granddad was for many years a JP (Justice of the Peace), jokingly maintaining he was always a JP as, being James Pratt, these were of course his initials. JPs were lay people of good character, empowered to administer criminal or civil justice in minor cases, and Granddad would hear such cases at the Hornby Petty Sessions.

In serving his fellow workers and community, Granddad was doing more than fulfilling the ideals of the old Primitive Methodists; he was obeying the exhortation of the Lord Jesus. "You are the salt of the earth. You are the light of the world.

45

Let your light so shine before men that they may see your good works and glorify your Father in heaven."[5] He was also following in the steps of believers such as William Wilberforce, Elizabeth Fry and George Muller, whose evangelical faith had a social conscience.

Sadly with some, the 'social gospel' became the 'gospel', and works became more important than repentance and faith. Granddad never fell into this trap, and whilst ministering to humanity's physical and material needs, he always kept before him the supreme importance of the soul.

An overreaction against the social gospel has resulted in many sincere believers shying away from any political or trade union involvement. This has meant that devoid of Christian influence, political parties and trade unions have become increasingly secular. To be 'in' the world and not 'of' the world is still a necessary but not an easy balance for any child of God.

---

[5] Matthew 5:13,14,16

6

Hobbies and Interests

BEING A COUNCILLOR AND A TRADE UNION OFFICIAL meant there were meetings to attend most weeks, and so whilst Granddad had other interests, the leisure time he could allocate to them was always minimal. This ensured that no pastime ever became a consuming passion, which can be a danger for believers today.

I am not sure that Granddad ever actually watched a football or cricket match, but he was interested in these two sports. At 5 p.m. on a Saturday, the radio was switched on for *Sports Report* and the introductory music – 'Out of the Blue' – was possibly the first piece of secular music I ever became familiar with. The Everton result was the one Granddad particularly looked out for, having delivered milk in the streets near Goodison Park.

It was Granddad who nurtured my interest in cricket, as each April, he bought my brother and me a copy of *Playfair Annual*. First published in 1948, this pocket-sized book, with its review of the previous season and the potted biographies and career records of current players, was avidly read and whetted our appetite for the coming season. Interestingly, the first test match ever played in England was in 1880 – the year of Granddad's birth.

In the previously mentioned *Methodist Preachers' Who's Who* for 1934, cycling was listed as one of Granddad's interests. However, I doubt if he ever just went 'for a ride'. For years, his bicycle was the means by which he got to preaching appointments or to the homes of the people he was visiting.

I recall seeing Granddad on his bicycle, but my abiding memory is of him on his motorbike. One day, he rode to our home in Morecambe, but unknown to us, the motorbike had broken down within minutes of him setting back for Caton. Instead of seeking help, he walked back the seven miles, riding freewheel downhill when this was possible. Perhaps not the wisest thing to do, but still quite an achievement for a diabetic man in his eighties.

In the evening, my grandparents would sometimes have a game of dominoes or draughts. Dominoes was my grand-mother's favourite, bringing out her competitive spirit, whilst Granddad was always hard to beat at draughts. As a teenager, chess was to become my passion, but it was draughts with Granddad which first instigated my interest in board games.

Throwing rubber hoopla rings onto a wooden board was another game in which Granddad participated. When rings got lost or passed their best, I remember they were sometimes replaced by rings that had been used to make jars airtight – a simple pleasure but one which Granddad greatly enjoyed.

My grandparents never had a television set, and Granddad's first real introduction to this medium came towards the end of his life when he was staying with my uncle. I remember how amused he had been by Harry Worth and his famous 'shop window' scene. That was the age of gentle and innocent comedy, far removed from what often passes for humour today.

Not possessing a television, they regularly listened to the news on the radio, as well as the shipping and weather forecasts. The only other programmes I can recall them tuning in to were *The Archers* and *Have A Go*. Still today, I cannot hear 'Barwick Green' – the signature tune of *The Archers* – without being transported back to 43 Hornby Road, Caton. My grandparents never missed this "everyday story of country folk", but whether they would have approved of today's storylines is perhaps debatable.

Have a Go ran from 1946 to 1967, and at its peak, it had twenty million listeners. The programme was presented by Yorkshireman Wilfred Pickles and at village halls throughout the country; ordinary people talked about their lives and memories. By answering simple quiz questions, contestants were able to win a small amount of money. Wilfred Pickles used some catchphrases such as "Are you courting?" and "Have you ever had an embarrassing moment?", all which came into popular parlance.

Granddad was also a keen reader. He did not possess an extensive library but possessed a number of Bible commentaries and Christian books. Some of these I inherited, and they proved most useful in my early days as a preacher. I benefitted greatly from a small book, *Bible Readings in the Gospel of Mark* by Henry Thorne. The author was the travelling secretary for the English National Committee of the YMCA, and the book has now been out of print for many years.

The *Jamieson-Fausset-Brown Bible Commentary*, first published in 1871, had been presented to Granddad in appreciation of fifty years preaching at Caton Baptist Church. The commentary was issued with the prayer, "May the Lord who caused the Holy Scriptures to be written for our learning, bless the effort and make it an instrument towards the conversion of sinners and the edification of saints to the glory of His great Name and the hastening of His kingdom. Amen." I have no doubt the prayer was answered in my grandfather's ministry and I can only hope in some measure in my own ministry as well.

Besides books, Granddad also enjoyed reading newspapers and Christian periodicals, which each week he passed on to us. The ones I remember are the *News Chronicle* (absorbed into the *Daily Mail* in 1960), *Lancaster Guardian*, *Christian Herald*, *Sunday Companion* and the *Joyful News*. The latter had been begun by Thomas Champness in 1883 and was taken over by Samuel Chadwick, his successor at Cliff College.

Joyful News ceased to exist in 1963, but the first copy intriguingly set out the paper's ethos and purpose.

What we want:

1) News of recent revivals;
2) Stories of remarkable conversions;
3) Answers to prayer;
4) Illustrations of providence.

What we do not want:

1) Politics;
2) Controversy;
3) Connexional Finance.

I remember seeing copies of *Joyful News*, but I was too young to ever really appreciate the paper.

The Dalesman was one of Granddad's favourite magazines, as with its emphasis on rural communities, it highlighted different people and places in Yorkshire. As a boy, I was fascinated by the cartoon figure Old Amos who, each month, dished out quotable advice. If Amos was old then, he must be quite ancient now, as today he is still sharing his wisdom with readers of the magazine.

I inherited my grandfather's love of books, magazines and sometimes, to my wife's despair, his love of newspapers. The *Daily Mail* is delivered to my door, and it has always been my custom when visiting a new area to buy the local newspaper. Pat put her foot down when, having mentioned this one Sunday from the pulpit, members of the congregation began to provide me with newspapers bought on their travels.

Another abiding memory of Granddad is of him putting on his overalls and proceeding to chop wood. 43 Hornby Road only ever had coal fires, and there was the constant need for kindling. Every Wednesday in Morecambe, having had a drink of tea, it was overalls on and into the garage to chop wood. Rather than being just a necessary chore, I suspect that Granddad found it to be a pleasurable exercise. He enjoyed working with wood, and my first train was built by him, with the wheels being made out of bobbins. Later, not being able to afford a cricket bat, he shaped one for me, and with it, I scored a host of runs in 'test matches' against my brother.

There was a photograph of Granddad in the *Lancaster Guardian* on his eightieth birthday with the heading "He's no sleeper". In the photograph, he is sawing a railway sleeper – a piece of timber used to support and keep rails in place. The accompanying article emphasised Granddad's busy lifestyle; hence, the title of the article.

I do not recall Granddad being a keen gardener – any interest being in fruit and vegetables rather than flowers. This was demonstrated by his unconventional use of the front garden where, somewhat to some family members' disapproval, he grew potatoes! His back garden was more orthodox with apple trees and a profusion of gooseberry, blackcurrant and red currant bushes. Each autumn, I helped him pick the berries and much appreciated the taste of the red currants.

In his garden, Granddad had two sheds, and being something of a hoarder, these became an Aladdin's cave. "I won't throw it away – it might come in useful" was his mantra, and consequently, nails, screws, washers, knives, door handles, badges, pens, pencils, books, bills, papers, a Gladstone bag etc. were all to be found in drawers and cupboards. Today, those huts would have been the ideal location for a TV antique programme.

Granddad was a cat lover, and I cannot remember when he was without a feline companion. Friendly cats, feisty cats, a Manx cat and even a cat with three legs found refuge in his home. Living by the busy A683, cats were often knocked down and killed, and retrieving them, Granddad would bury them in the garden.

Grandma tolerated cats, but they did not mean to her what they meant to him. On a bitter winter's night, cats would be purring in front of a roaring fire until the clock struck half past eight. That was the cue for Grandma to pick up a cat and unceremoniously put it out of the backdoor – not too many home comforts for Grandma's cats, but they always seemed none the worse for their 'night on the tiles'.

And so, Granddad did have hobbies and interests, but they were always secondary to his work for the Master. The Apostle Paul said, "This one thing I do," and this, with so many believers of his generation, was Granddad's testimony. Their Christianity was no hobby but something all-consuming.

7

43 Hornby Road

MOST HOUSES IN THE 1950s AND 1960s WERE NOT primarily known for comfort or luxury, and this was true of 43 Hornby Road, where new furniture and appliances were almost unknown. In their later years, my uncle bought heaters to help them warm the house, but to his frustration, they were rarely switched on. In winter, they were certainly needed, because without central heating, the house was often cold and draughty.

However, having known hard, austere times, there was no possibility of extravagance characterising their twilight years. Lights were never switched on or curtains drawn until it was dark outside. I remember peering through the window and just about being able to see them against the glow of the fire.

For much of the year, the only rooms in use were the living room, the kitchen, a bedroom and the bathroom. As with many families of that era, the front room (sometimes known as the parlour or sitting room) was traditionally reserved for Christmas and special occasions. For me, it was a 'no-go area' until my grandparents started using it as a downstairs bedroom.

With an outside toilet, there was no need to go upstairs, and I can only remember once venturing on to the first floor. It must have been autumn time, as the back bedroom was festooned with apples, recently picked from the fruit trees in the garden. Neither do I recall ever using the front door, as access to the house was gained via the backdoor – known colloquially as the 'tradesman's entrance'.

Whilst researching the book, to my surprise, I discovered that what I have just written is not strictly true. I was born in the village of Melling – six miles from Caton – and apparently, my first address was 43 Hornby Road. At the time, my parents were waiting for a house to become available and so they were staying with my grandparents. Consequently, rooms unknown to me as a child may have been occupied by me as a baby.

Today with fridges and freezers, we have little problem keeping food fresh and safe to eat. Things were somewhat different in my grandparent's day when the reliance was not on 'use by' or 'sell by' dates but rather on the look, feel and smell of the food. Whilst easy to tell when milk had gone sour, bread dry or cheeses mouldy, guessing when meat or fish had been kept too long was much more challenging. I can recall both my grandparents having mild food poisoning after eating chicken.

In the 1950s, before the advent of supermarkets, village communities were dependent on mobile grocery shops delivering to the door, and this was how my grandparents purchased most of their provisions. Who would have thought that delivery vans would ever have been needed again, but with groceries increasingly being ordered on the internet, they are now a common sight.

As with most people of their generation, my grandparents had a simple fare, though some of their meals might cause raised eyebrows today. My grandfather was fond of the 'frying pan' and also particularly partial to cheese. One of his favourite snacks was 'bannock' and cheese. Bannocks seem to have been a different food in different parts of the country, but for Granddad, it was just a pastry bun baked in the oven. My personal recollection is that whilst it was scrumptious with butter when first baked, it soon became dry and crumbly.

Despite what some might have considered in parts an unhealthy diet, Grandma and Granddad lived to be ninety-one and eighty-eight respectively. I am no medic, but this may have been due to being physically active and having a relatively healthy war and post-war diet. Food rationing from 1940 to 1954 prohibited any opportunity for overindulgence.

After he retired, Granddad was diagnosed with diabetes, and for several years, he had to inject himself morning and evening. It was not a pleasant procedure but something he did every day without complaining. Granddad always had a lump of sugar in his waistcoat pocket – something to be taken if his sugar levels fell. I can only remember one occasion when he fell into a 'diabetic coma' and needed hospital admission. As a result of his condition, I was introduced to diabetic jam, jelly and sweets, but as a boy, they were nothing that I relished.

Another childhood memory is of the number of chiming clocks in the house. Every quarter of an hour, there was a cacophony of sound as clocks of different shapes and sizes rang out the time. Some of the chimes were slow, but others rapid as though they were trying to overtake the chimes that had gone before. I presume they chimed throughout the night, but with Grandma being deaf, she probably never heard them, and as for Granddad, being used to the 'bells' of the signal box, no doubt the chimes were music to his ear.

Granddad was a stickler for time, but it was his pocket watch, not the house clocks, which was his constant companion. It used to be said, "Once a railwayman, always a railwayman," and this was so true when Granddad told you the time. It was never "nearly half-past six" but rather "twenty-nine and a half minutes after six". Poignantly, before he died, he handed his well-loved pocket watch to my uncle, saying, "You have this – I won't be needing it anymore." Sensing his home call, he knew that his time on earth was about to be exchanged for the timeless days of heaven.

Granddad, although a cat-lover, did have two dogs in the house. As in many homes at that time, there were two Staffordshire dog figurines on the mantlepiece – a matching pair of facing pottery spaniels. On marrying my Scottish wife, I was told that they were called 'Wally dogs' north of the border.

The most important thing about a house is that it should be a home, and 43 Hornby Road certainly fitted that criteria. It came to life every Christmas Day when my grandparents hosted a family party. Up to a dozen gathered early in the evening for a meal and games. On one memorable occasion, my uncle secreted a tape recorder – a relatively new invention in the 1950s – next to my grandma's chair. Unaware of its presence, grandma was quite vocal, but to our amusement, when the tape was played back, she refused to believe that the voice was hers and wanted to know who was speaking. The party never finished until after midnight, and as a boy, it was the one time in the year when I went to bed on a different day to the one in which I had got up.

It was a home and patently a Christian home, and as an unconverted youngster, this impacted me. On the wall, there was a print of 'The Broad and Narrow Way' – a picture which can still be seen in older church vestries. I understand the print became well known when an Open-Air Mission evangelist used it to illustrate a sermon on Matthew 7:13-14.

On the left of the print, there was the 'Way to Perdition' with theatres, ballrooms, taverns etc. and on the right, the 'Way of Salvation' with churches and Sunday schools. With numerous texts, one path led to heaven and the other to hell. I can still remember, as a child, being disturbed by this graphic presentation of the gospel.

The riverside at Philippi was a place "where prayer was customarily made"[6], which was true of my grandparents' home. Whenever we were preparing to leave, Granddad would say, "We will just have a word of prayer," and getting to our knees, he would commend us all to our Father in heaven. Posture may not be the most important thing in prayer, but 'bowing the knee' is a reminder that we pray to a sovereign, majestic God.

In later years, as his memory failed, we would sometimes have to prompt him when he could not recall the name of a family member. When young, you never envisage that happening to you, but I am now at an age when it is by no means an unknown occurrence.

It was a godly home but, like every Christian home, not perfect. Even with hearing aids, Grandmother was almost stone deaf, and whilst this was a severe trial for her, it was also a trial for Granddad. Many an evening, his voice was hoarse, as throughout the day, he had tried to 'get through' to Grandma. To add to his woes, Grandma was convinced the problem was not so much her deafness but rather his muttering. "If he would only speak up, I could hear him," was her complaint.

Her frustration was understandable as prior to a cataract operation and being deaf, she was also blind. Granddad was incredibly kind, taking her rebukes with good humour, and never once did I see him lose his patience. However, the best of homes is but a pale shadow of that heavenly home where "the

---

[6] Acts 16:13

eyes of the blind shall be opened and the ears of the deaf shall be unstopped"[7].

---

[7] Isaiah 35:5

8

Miscellaneous Memories

CATON STATION, WHERE GRANDDAD WORKED FOR almost forty years, was on the Lancaster Green Ayre to Wennington railway line. It opened in 1850 but fell victim to the Beeching axe and closed in 1961. The line ran behind my grandparents' home and contributed to a childhood memory. When we were travelling to Leeds, my grandparents would wave a white sheet from a bedroom window as the train passed by.

One such journey must have been in January 1956 because I distinctly remember having the very first copy of the *Beezer* comic with me. It costs 3d, and inside, there was a whiz-bang – a piece of card that banged when you threw the insides out. And so, the whiz-bang was waved in response to the white sheet.

After closure, the station was modified as a private dwelling, whilst the goods shed is now Caton Catholic Church. Pleasingly, the dismantled line between Caton and Lancaster has been preserved as a cycle-path and footpath. When we lived in Ingleton, we often walked this disused line, and I never did so without thinking of Granddad.

Every Wednesday, my grandparents spent the day with us in Morecambe, but the journey was made by bus and not by train. Caton was only eight miles away, but it involved two bus journeys, and once in Morecambe, there was a half-mile walk to our home. During school holidays, my brother and I would be watching out for them, and many times, we were convinced that Granddad had come on his own. There was no sight of Grandma, but then, as Granddad arrived at the front door, she would come round the corner, supported by her trusty walking stick. Happily together for over sixty years, I could never quite fathom why they did not walk together on a Wednesday. At other times, they often linked arms – Granddad saying, with a smile, "We are Lincoln City."

Granddad was in the habit of handing out gospel leaflets, and yet this commendable but neglected form of evangelism did not always gain him the favour of Grandma. "He's ruining his pockets" was her complaint, as his overcoat bulged with tracts. Ruined pockets, however, would not have caused Granddad too much concern as he was never a 'dedicated follower of fashion'.

My mother recalled a rare occasion when he had bought a new suit and the trousers came with a crease. Not wanting anyone to know he had bought a new suit, the first thing he did was rub out the creases. Years after retirement, he was still wearing the jackets and trousers he had worn as a signalman. 'With food and raiment', he was content, and I suspect even more contented, the plainer the food and the raiment.

My grandparents never went away on holiday, but in their later years, they came each August and spent ten days with us in Morecambe. This was a necessary break for them both but especially for Granddad, who increasingly had become Grandma's carer. His meals were prepared for him, and he could devote more time to some of those things he really enjoyed: chopping wood and home visiting.

On the mantlepiece – not a word often used today – Granddad would place several piles of coins, and every morning, taking a pile of coins, we would go to the newsagent and buy his *Daily Mail*. With the money left over at the end of their stay, we were able to treat ourselves to ice cream.

Mention of the *Daily Mail* reminds me of another way in which, during his annual break, we were of help to Granddad. When at home, except for Sunday, he read the paper every day to Grandma. As previously stated, this was not an easy task, as Grandma was very deaf and things had to be repeated many times. It is for this reason that August 1963 and the great train robbery is entrenched in my memory. For several mornings, I read to Grandma what had happened and the progress being made in trying to catch the villains.

The Cliff College 'trekkers' held meetings on Morecambe promenade in August, and these services were a highlight of Granddad's visit. On a Friday night, there was a Gospel Rally at Parliament Street Methodist Church. This was a special joy to Granddad, as Parliament Street was an old 'Prim' chapel, and the speakers were often Cliff evangelists, such as Tom Butler or Herbert Silverwood.

Methodism was born in song, and the Friday night meeting was enlivened by the singing of Cliff College choruses. A lady commented that when Granddad preached, his voice was "as clear as a bell" but sadly, being tone-deaf, this could not be said of his singing. Nevertheless, he loved the Methodist Hymnbook with 'When we walk with the Lord in the light of his Word' being his favourite.

My grandparents were born and bred in the Yorkshire Dales, and this was reflected in their conversation. Sadly, today, due to greater mobility, the media and the emphasis on standard English in education, there is the danger of local dialects dying out. This was not the case in past years when many never moved away from where they had been born and were not influenced by modern means of communication. It is true that, as a young man, Granddad had spent time away, but not long enough to abandon the language of the Dales altogether.

It was, therefore, often "nah then" (hello) when we met and "si-thi" (goodbye) when we parted. As boys, coming in from football and cricket games, the instruction was "sit thissen down, tha's been laiking all day" (sit down, have a rest, you've been playing all day). If someone was in good health, they were "champion" or in "fine fettle"; if in reasonable health, they were "fair to middlin", but if they were not too well, then they were "nobbut middlin".

I assumed, as a child, that these words and phrases were in common usage, but I soon came to learn otherwise. To their amusement, I now use some of these phrases with my own grandchildren, but I am not expecting them to become fluent in the dialect of their great, great grandfather.

I remember Granddad's dialect, but far more than that, I remember his mischievous sense of humour. Although my grandparents visited every Wednesday, there was still a letter from them on a Saturday. This was not unusual in the 1950s and 1960s, with so few people being on the telephone. Grandma wrote the letter, but it always included, for the grandchildren, a joke from Granddad. Contrary to the popular saying, Granddad proved you could be 'heavenly minded' and do 'earthly good'. That is why, with great affection, I remember him as a God-fearing man but also as a fun-loving grandfather.

9

Sermon Notes

I INHERITED A MILADY CONFECTIONERY TIN WHICH contained Granddad's sermon notes, written on any piece of paper or cardboard that was available. For example, I found notes on the back of a letter for an Independent Hearing Aid Consultant and a card advertising "New Joker Safety Razor Blades". The notes for Eph.1:3 were on a receipt card – Ref. No. 13248 – from a ladies' clothing company: "We beg to acknowledge with thanks receipt of your esteemed order, which is receiving attention." It is quite a contrast today when sermon notes are typed and then saved on computers more often than not.

During his seventy years of lay ministry, Granddad preached at least once from all sixty-six books of the Bible. This is a testimony to his worth as a preacher – not just expounding familiar texts but seeking to preach the 'whole counsel of God'. It has been a joy to read these sermon notes, and it is a privilege to bring a sample to a wider audience.

1 Kings 18:30: "He repaired the altar of the Lord that was broken down."

Elijah laid down a challenge. Before a blessing could come, before the blessing could fall, the broken-

down altars must be repaired. In the Old Testament, the altar was the outward expression of an inward experience. The altar here had fallen into disuse, and this represents the spiritual condition of God's people. Today, you and I have finished with external altars; there are altars just the same in all our hearts. Is there a broken altar in your life?

1) *The Altar of Prayer.*

True prayer is hard work. It involves the spirit, mind and body, but it is the secret of all spiritual success.

2) *The Altar of Sacrifice.*

Too often, we want the easy life, not the life of sacrifice.

3) *The Altar of Personal Devotion.*

We need to love the Master, not only for what He gives but for His own dear sake. Is Christ real to you? Is He precious?

Nehemiah 13:11: "Why is the house of God forsaken?"

The words of Nehemiah to the returning exiles, written after the backsliding and downfall of Jerusalem. God's blessing had been enjoyed during David and Solomon's days, but now, their religious life had decayed, and the Temple was desolate.

1) *Many churches are forsaken by God.*

The word 'Ichabod' can be written across them. Because of the sins of the people, the glory has departed. The church may be full of people, financially prosperous with good music and preaching, and yet – like the Laodiceans – still be forsaken by God.

2) *Many churches are forsaken by the saints.*

God is present with the faithful few, but others are absent from many of the services. They blame the preacher or some other members of the church for real or imaginary grievances. They are engaged in anything but prayer.

3) *Many churches are forsaken by the people.*

Only 10% of the nation are now regular attendees – where are the 90% who have forsaken the house of God? They do not come because of materialism and pleasure. Under Nehemiah, there was a measure of revival and a return to the neglected Word of God. We need the same, and prayer is the key.

Job 19:25: "I know that my Redeemer lives."

1) *A word of assurance: "I know"*

We need a knowledge that gives us a confidence.

Paul: "I know Whom I have believed."

Blind man: "But this one thing I know."

Apostle John: "We know we have passed from death to life."

2) A word of deliverance: "Redeemer"

To redeem means to buy back. One who pays the price. Jesus paid the price of our redemption at Calvary.

3) A word of triumph: "lives"

Calvary is not a defeat but a victory. The seal, the guard and the sepulchre could not hold Jesus. He ever lives.

4) A word of possession: "my"

Take away the personal pronoun and what is left? Do we possess Christ or merely profess Him? Do we use Him, or does He use us?

The Lord is MY Keeper. MY Redeemer. MY Coming King.

Psalm 51:10: "Create in me a clean heart, O God and renew a steadfast spirit within me."

1) "Create"

Wonderful word. Only God can create. We remake, remodel, reconstruct, but only God can create. Without Him, we are helpless and hopeless.

2) "in me"

Others may have sinned and gone wrong, but the Psalmist was concerned about the sin in his own heart.

3) "a clean heart"

Sin had defiled, degraded, and deluded.

"The heart is deceitful."

"Out of the heart are the issues of life."

"Wash me and I shall be whiter than snow."

4) "O God"

Only the Lord can do this, and He will.

5) "renew a steadfast spirit within me"

If we have been un-Christlike, uncharitable, unkind, unjust, or unloving, we need to confess our wrong spirit and make a clean breast of our failures.

Four Simple Prayers

1) Save me.

Peter's prayer for salvation
Matthew 14:30

2) Keep me.

Jabez's prayer for preservation
1 Chronicles 4:10

3) Teach me.

David's prayer for instruction
Psalm 27:11

4) Send me.

Isaiah's prayer for guidance
Isaiah 6:8

Matthew 5:13: "You are the salt of the earth."

1) *Salt has cleansing properties.*

2) *Salt is great as a relish.* Job 6:6. Many lives around us are flavourless.

3) *Salt is thirst-inducing.* Jesus said, "If any man thirst, let him come unto Me and drink." Many need to be made thirsty.

4) *Salt is a preserver* – what a terrible place this world would be if there were no Christians and no Holy Spirit.

Matthew 17:14-21: Post-Transfiguration

1) Work among the multitude is to be the outcome of communion on the mount.

2) The need of the multitude makes necessary communion on the mount.

3) We fail among the multitude for want of communion on the mount.

"He climbs a mountain in vain who leaves it as he finds it."

Mark 14:8: "She has done what she could. She has come beforehand to anoint My body for burial."

What a commendation:

1) *The gift was spontaneous.* Divine love was bubbling in her heart.

2) *The gift was self-sacrificing.* She gave what cost her something.

3) *The gift was singular.* Not a common thing to do. It is a love that dared to be different.

4) *The gift was seasonable.* Calvary was just ahead.

Acts 8:26-39: "He went on his way rejoicing." (v.39)

Why?

1) Because an evangelist obeyed the Lord (v.29).

2) Because an evangelist did his best for a small congregation (v.26).

3) Because he was willing to be taught by one poorer than himself (v.27).

4) Because the atonement of Jesus was preached (vs.32-35).

5) Because he had faith in a substitute (v.37).

6) Because he was baptised (v.38).

Acts 8-10

Three conversions in Acts representing three continents and three races.

1) Acts 8	Ethiopian Eunuch	Africa	Shem
2) Acts 9	Saul of Tarsus	Asia	Ham
3) Acts 10	Cornelius	Europe	Japheth

Acts 12:12: The House of Mary

1) Mary's home was a place where needy ones could come.

2) Mary's home was a place for prayer.

3) Mary's home was a place where others were inspired to serve. For example, John Mark.

Have we a home like this?

Acts 17:18: "...he preached to them Jesus and the resurrection."

1) *The preacher.*

Paul, a man of learning but now converted and commissioned to preach the Gospel.

2) *The preparation.*

v.16: "At Athens, his spirit was stirred in him, when he saw the city wholly given to idolatry."

3) *The pulpit.*

v.17. "Synagogue"

v.17. "Market Place"

v.18. "Mars Hill"

4) *The people.*

v.18. "The Epicureans" were high-minded rationalists who believed in pleasure. 'The Stoics' extolled virtue but denied human responsibility and future judgement.

Paul preached Jesus – His ministry, His crucifixion, His resurrection – either light to brighten the tomb or a token of future judgement.

The result. vs.32-34. Some mocked. Some hesitated. Some believed. His mission was no failure, for some did believe. Do you believe in Jesus and the resurrection?

Acts 26:18 (Paul's message to the Gentiles): "...to open their eyes, in order to turn them from darkness to light and the power of Satan to God, that they may receive forgiveness of sins and an inheritance among those who are sanctified by faith in Me."

1) *Revelation.* *To open their eyes.*

2) *Repentance.* *To turn them from darkness to light.*

3) *Release.* *From the power of Satan to God.*

4) *Remission.* *Receive forgiveness of sin.*

5) *Riches.* *An inheritance.*

6) *Reserved.* *Among those who are sanctified.*

Hebrews 2:3: "...so great a salvation."

How great and why?

1) *Because it costs a great price. Bethlehem. Nazareth. Gethsemane. Calvary.*

2) *Because it brings a great change. Sinners – Saints. Selfish – Generous. Boastful – Humble. Liars – Truthful.*

3) *Because it meets the needs of all. Matthew the publican, Mary Magdalene, Nicodemus, woman at the well.*

Hebrews 2:9: "...we see Jesus ... crowned with glory and honour..."

Four aspects of His coronation.

1) *The backward look.*

Jesus crowned on the cross. It was a crown of thorns, but Jesus did His mightiest work on the cross. That through death He might destroy him who had the power of death, that is the devil (Heb.2:14).

2) *The upward look.*

Jesus was crowned in heaven. Far above all principality and power and might and dominion and every name that is named not only in this age but also in that which is to come (Eph.1:21).

3) *The onward look.*

Jesus crowned on earth. He returns as the Lord of lords and King of kings (Rev.17:14).

4) The inward look.

Jesus crowned in our hearts. In your hearts, enthrone Him.

(A believer was able to recall this sermon some fifty years after he had heard it preached.)

Revelation 1:9-10: "I was on the island ... I was in the Spirit."

1) The contrast between Circumstances and Character.

John – on Patmos but in the Spirit.

John Bunyan – in Bedford Gaol but in the Spirit.

Martin Luther – in the castle walls at Wartburg but in the Spirit.

2) The contrast between Limitation and Liberty.

Despite restrictions, John was free in the Spirit.

3) The contrast between Tremble and Trust.

Patmos was guarded by water – a sign of unrest. The wicked are like the troubled sea. There is consolation in the Spirit.

4) The contrast between Loneliness and Love.

Alone "on the isle" but not in the Spirit: "The Father is with me."

A number of Granddad's sermon notes were written on the back of a Moor Lane Circuit, Lancaster 'Order of Service' sheet. There was always a 'Hymn for Children' and a 'Children's Address' on the Morning Order, and I include two such addresses.

American Flag

A gentleman was visiting a school in America, and the schoolmaster said, "This boy is one of my brightest scholars, and he will do a drawing for you."

The drawing being completed, the visitor said, "What is it?"

"Sir," the boy replied, "it is my country's flag. The Stars and Stripes. The American flag."

"No, it isn't," the gentleman said. "You have only drawn nine stripes. You need to add four more stripes before you can call it the Flag of the United States. 13 stripes representing 13 colonies."

Have you left out what should never be left out?

1) Do you ever leave out grace at meals?

2) Do you ever forget to say your prayers?

3) Do you omit to say thank you or sorry?

4) Have you left Jesus out of your life?

Isaac Watts

One morning, at family prayers, little Isaac opened his eyes and saw a wee mouse. It ran across the library floor and up the bell-rope, which Isaac's father pulled when he called his servants. There, the mouse remained, solemnly looking down as the family said their prayers.

Little Isaac laughed out loud and was later rebuked by his father, who asked, "Why did you laugh during prayers?"

"I couldn't help it," said Isaac. "I saw a mouse, and I have written a verse about it."

This is what Isaac had written. "There was a mouse for want of stairs. Who climbed a rope to say his prayers."

"Huh," said his father, without a smile on his face, "writing verses is a waste of time; you must keep your mind on more serious things" – no more verses for poor little Isaac when his head was full of them.

But encouraged by his mother, he became a great hymn-writer, and he wrote two of the hymns we are singing this morning: 'Come ye that love the Lord' and 'Jesus shall reign'.

John Stott said, "The preachers who have influenced their generation have all borne witness to conscientious preparation." These notes are surely a testimony to Granddad's diligent and thoughtful preparation, and I am struck by his clear sermon structure. Some sermons can be like a magical mystery tour –

you set out not knowing where you are going, and you arrive at the end not knowing where you have been or how you got there. Therefore, a clear structure with helpful headings is a necessary safeguard and helps to establish the truths of the sermon in the minds of the hearers.

There is a preparation of the sermon, but if preaching is to be effective, the preacher must also be prepared. "For Ezra had prepared his heart to seek the Law of the Lord and to do it and to teach statutes and ordinances in Israel."[8] For many years, on a Saturday night, Grandma would go to her sister's house down the road, while Granddad spent time in prayer. A challenge to all who preach: the sermon might be prepared, but am I?

---

[8] Ezra 7:10

10

Granddad's Legacy

WE ALL LEAVE A LEGACY, BUT THE MOST VALUABLE legacy we can pass on to our children and grandchildren is not material but spiritual. And because Granddad was 'rich in faith', his legacy far exceeded, in importance, any temporary inheritance of money or property.

Lay preacher, Sunday School Superintendent, leader of Christian Endeavour, conscientious visitor... Granddad spent a lifetime serving the Lord Jesus without any desire for financial reward. He was motivated only by a love for the Lord, a passion for souls and a desire to build up and encourage the people of God.

However, I sometimes wonder whether he would have been able to do in the twenty-first century what he did in the twentieth. I am concerned about the professionalising of Christian ministry. Children and teenage work is now often the prerogative of the trained youth worker, and visiting is the responsibility of the trained counsellor. Today, would a railway signalman with just a basic education be acceptable to the church, or would he be made to feel unqualified and inadequate?

Lest I be misunderstood, I am not decrying education or training, and I would emphasise that the great need is always for excellence in ministry. Indeed, this was Apostle Paul's emphasis: "Be an example to the believers in word, in conduct, in love, in spirit, in faith, in purity. Till I come, give attention to reading, to exhortation, to doctrine. Do not neglect the gift that is in you."[9] Whether leading worship, preaching the Word, ministering to children and young people, or visiting the needy, we must always strive for excellence and treat every part of our life and ministry with the utmost spiritual care.

And so, whilst we do need education, training and professionalism, these things are no substitute for persistent prayer, a hunger for God and a devotion to Christ. "When they saw the boldness of Peter and John and perceived that they were uneducated and untrained men, they marvelled. And they realised that they had been with Jesus."[10]

Peter and John caused the Jewish Sanhedrin to marvel, for they were Galilean fishermen with no formal education but they had the one essential qualification for ministry: "...they had been with Jesus." It would be sad, even tragic, if this essential qualification were ever to be considered as being of secondary importance when compared to formal training and education. Spending much time with Jesus was the secret of my grandfather's lifetime of effective service.

Alcohol, cigarettes, playing cards, pubs, cinemas, theatres – these were all out of bounds for my grandparents, whilst Sunday observance and two services on the Lord's Day were the accepted norm. Sadly, today, believers with such convictions can be considered old-fashioned and accused of legalism.

---

[9] 1 Timothy 4:12-14
[10] Acts 4:13

I can never recall Granddad lecturing anyone about his personal convictions – he rather led by example. And his example showed it was possible to be happy and content without indulging in such things. Granddad was always good company, and there was never anything dull or judgmental about him.

I would not be hypocritical and pretend I have always adhered to my grandfather's convictions, but I do wonder if my more relaxed attitude has contributed to a general laxity observable in some churches today. Are some not in danger of giving the impression that Christians need to be converted to the world, rather than the world converted to Christ?

Bishop J.C. Ryle was conscious of this danger when he wrote in 1878:

> There is a widely-spread desire to make things pleasant in religion – to saw off the edges and corners of the cross, and to avoid as far as possible, self-denial. On every side, we hear professing Christians declaring loudly that we must not be "narrow and exclusive", and there is no harm in many things which the holiest saints of old thought bad for their souls. That we may go anywhere, and do anything, and spend our time in anything, and read anything, and keep any company, and plunge into anything, and all the while be exceptionally good Christians – this is the maxim of thousands. In a day like this, I think it good to raise a warning voice, and invite attention to the teaching of God's Word. It is written in that Word: "Come out and be separate."

In no way did Granddad turn his back on the world, being a parish and district councillor, a union official and a source of help to anyone in his village. 'Salt' and 'light' as Jesus commanded. He did, however, turn his back on worldly entertainment and pastimes, and as a Bible believer, I cannot say he was mistaken.

When Granddad started preaching towards the end of the nineteenth century, Methodism had almost 900,000 members, but at the time of his death in 1968, this had reduced to around 650,000. The decline since has been even more rapid, and in 2020, the membership stood at 173,000.

Sociological factors, including two world wars, undoubtedly had a significant impact, but Granddad would have pinpointed other reasons. Theological liberalism and the social gospel began to emerge in the late 1800s and the early 1900s, and laid the groundwork for what was to happen in the future.

In my grandfather's later years, the denomination embarked on the Anglican-Methodist Conversations, with the hope of reuniting the two churches. Beginning in 1955, the proposals were accepted by the Methodist Conference in 1968 but were not accepted by the Anglican communion. This desire for ecumenism never found favour with Granddad.

In 1966, at the National Assembly of Evangelicals, Dr Martyn Lloyd-Jones called on evangelicals to withdraw from denominations in which they were "united to the people who deny and are opposed to the essential matters of salvation". A year or two after Granddad's death, there were Methodists in North Lancashire who responded to the call, and if this had happened earlier, I am certain he would have identified with them.

It is a testimony to the Lord's keeping power that Granddad remained faithful to biblical truth when many departed from it. Higher criticism and theological liberalism never eroded his confidence in the infallibility of the Scriptures. I am reminded of the words of the Risen Christ to one of the seven churches: "You have a few names, even in Sardis, who have not defiled their garments; and they shall walk with Me in white for they are worthy."[11] Granddad was such a one, faithful to the Word and not defiled by those who would preach another gospel. This is a challenge to all believers of every age and generation.

Granddad was a man of prayer. He never came to our home or we to his without a "word of prayer" before departing. I know he prayed for my conversion, but on earth, he never saw the answer to his prayer, for it was some six months after his passing that I came to saving faith. However, that did not mean his prayers were unheard or unanswered.

David prayed, "But as for me, my prayer is to You, O Lord, in the acceptable time. O God, in the multitude of Your mercy, hear me in the truth of Your salvation."[12] Prayer is not always answered according to our timetable but according to the perfect timing of our Heavenly Father.

In a similar vein, Zacharias was told by the angel, "Your prayer is heard and your wife Elizabeth will bear you a son, and you shall call his name John."[13] I suspect that Zacharias had not prayed this prayer for many years "because Elizabeth was barren, and they were both well advanced in years"[14]. The

---

[11] Revelation 3:4
[12] Psalm 69:13
[13] Luke 1:13
[14] Luke 1:7

prayers offered years beforehand had not been in vain – they were answered 'in the acceptable time'.

Those prayers which, no doubt, Granddad had pleaded since the day of my birth, were answered six months after his death. What an incentive and encouragement that is to continue praying for children and grandchildren.

As all my Granddad memories are positive and wholesome, this is far from being a 'warts and all' biography. However, in no way am I inferring that he was a perfect man; but to prove this, there is no need to detail specific weaknesses and shortcomings. Surely, it is sufficient that as a young man, he trusted the Lord Jesus as his Saviour. Jesus said, "I did not come to call the righteous but sinners to repentance."[15] Granddad knew himself to be a sinner, so he repented and came to faith in Christ. And whilst he was not perfect – for no one is – he is perfect now. "We shall be like Him, for we shall see Him as He is."[16]

Granddad was a major influence upon me but also upon many others, as these two anecdotes illustrate. Speaking to a lady sometime ago, she commented, "Your grandfather was such a lovely man that, as a girl, I thought it was Jesus in the pulpit whenever he preached at the Mission."

The other comment came not from a believer but a 'man of the world', who was a work colleague of my brother. Knowing Jim was a Christian, he began to recall how, in his village of Caton, there had been a most remarkable man. "He had an aura about him. He was almost a saint."

"Was his name James Pratt?" enquired my brother.

---

[15] Matthew 9:13
[16] 1 John 3:2

"Yes, it was," responded his astonished colleague.

"That man," said my brother, "was my grandfather."

It brings to mind the words of George Mueller: "Worldly persons should be constrained to say of us, 'If ever there was a Christian upon earth, that man was one.'"

"A good man leaves an inheritance to his children's children."[17] The good man does indeed pass on to his children and grandchildren an inheritance far greater than any material wealth. My life has been so much richer because of the prayers, counsel and example of a godly grandfather, and for this, I give thanks to God.

---

[17] Proverbs 13:22

How Shall They Hear?
ISBN 978-1-911086-43-7

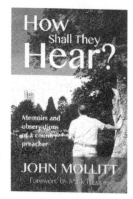

This collection of memoirs paints the life of a country preacher in broad strokes, through poignant anecdotes that will at times make you smile, at other times pause to reflect. John Mollitt was born in the Lune Valley, near to Lancaster. After an early career in banking and civil service, he served as Pastor of Ingleton Evangelical Church in North Yorkshire for thirty years. Then in 2009 he retired and began an itinerant preaching ministry.

A Life Worthwhile
ISBN 978-1-78815-656-1

Despite his complex medical needs and the doctors saying he would probably not reach the age of 10, John and Pat Mollitt's son Aaron lived life to the full for 28 years, bringing joy, hope and inspiration to those around him. This is a story of God's love expressed in the life of a family, and how their commitment to one another enabled them to overcome great challenges.

Truth in a Nutshell
ISBN 978-1-910197-77-6

More Truth in a Nutshell
ISBN 978-1-78815-553-3

These books of meditations each contain over 100 scriptures and anecdotes. Taken from the life and experiences of itinerant preacher, John Mollitt, each story illustrates a key lesson from the scripture being studied.